Human Potential

Human Potential

The search
for that
"something more"

Iain Scott

HPT Books

First published in 1994
by HPT Books

HPT Books is part of
The Human Potential Trust
The Oasis, Highbrook Lane
West Hoathly
Sussex RH19 4PL, England

A CIP catalogue record for this book is available
from the British Library.

Proceeds from the sale of this book, including
the author's royalties, will be used for charitable work.

ISBN 1-899131-01-9

Printed and bound by Biddles Ltd, Guildford, Surrey

CONTENTS

This book is dedicated to my wife, Sarah,
for all her love, understanding, and commitment.

PREFACE

Intercontinental air travel, astronauts walking on the moon, satellite television, and personal computers were all once beyond comprehension. Yet today these human achievements and much more are accepted as normal. It is strange to look back through history and remember that people once thought the Earth was flat; adventurous explorers were seriously warned that their ships would fall off the edge of the world if they went too far!

New discoveries change our perception and broaden our outlook. Knowledge is slowly replacing superstition and belief. First, there is the initial breakthrough - that moment of "eureka!" - when a fresh discovery is realised. This is followed by a more lengthy process of further exploration, general acceptance, and everyday application. The "new" then finally becomes the "normal".

The subject matter of this book deals with an exciting development that will certainly change our view of life. It will allow us to go way beyond our present limitations. This particular breakthrough is of fundamental importance because it is concerned with consciousness itself. It offers to unlock our hidden potential. The transformation of consciousness is the next major step forward in evolution. One day, this "new" and highly beneficial capacity will certainly be regarded as "normal" when it is eventually acquired by more and more of the human race.

I am 37 years of age and have a practical, "no-nonsense" approach to life. In the first section of this book, I have summarised my own unusual personal experiences. The second section begins by describing the effects of what we call "normal" consciousness. It then continues as a guide on how to gain the natural potential that lies within us all. I have purposely tried to keep my words simple and any explanations relevant to a wide audience. One final comment: believing what has happened to me is not necessary; what I describe later can be tested by anyone.

Iain Scott
Sussex, March 1994

SECTION ONE:

AN EXPLANATION

1

Prelude: a challenging experience

Childhood influences are known to determine behaviour later in life. Looking back, I can see that these early years made me receptive or ready for what was to eventually happen. Growing up as a boy, I enjoyed nature and outdoor hobbies. I was independently minded, keen to ask questions in the search for truth. Some people remarked that I seemed to have "an old head on young shoulders". But the most unusual influence of my youth occurred when I was 17 years old.

In 1974, between September 9th and December 20th, I was apparently contacted by extraterrestrials. There were three other people involved. The events that took place were real and not imagined. I carefully made a record of everything that happened, using audio cassette recordings and written notes. They encouraged and challenged each of us personally. We were never told nor asked to believe any philosophy. There was no discussion about knowledge of advanced technology. There seemed to be a purpose for the contact, although I still have a number of unanswered questions. We did not speak publicly about what had happened.

I have critically examined the events that took place, considering in turn the various possible interpretations. Was it all a hoax or hallucination? Was there some other normal or paranormal explanation? Both then and since, I have been unable to conclude that it was anything other than what it seemed: a genuine extraterrestrial contact.

I should make clear that I am highly sceptical about many of the cases claiming contact with beings from other planets. My opinion is that they are usually the result of fantasy and delusion. I first consider the conventional explanations before venturing into the unknown. If I am hard to convince, it is because of my wish to base any assessment on factual data and not on uncritical speculation.

2

Transformation:
the oneness experiences

Throughout the summer months of 1975 - having finished my "A" level school examinations - I spent much of the time alone, organising and typing up all the notes I had made of the events that took place between September 9th and December 20th. The extraterrestrial contact had left me understandably changed to some degree from how I was before. I could not deny nor forget what had happened. Day after day, thoughts and questions demanded an explanation.

Late one evening during this summer vacation, I experienced an astonishing expansion of consciousness. Timeless moments of ecstasy and oneness revealed a reality I had not previously considered. There was an intense awareness of the unity of everything and everyone. Life had an obvious meaning and purpose. This mental awareness was matched by an equally intense feeling of love, caring and belonging. I could see the problems facing our world and also a solution to them.

There was an incredible sense of needing to help others - not in any compulsive or unbalanced way, but rather because service was the natural thing to do. My selfish tendencies had effortlessly melted away, although I still retained an appreciation of individuality. There was no sense of separateness, only oneness.

My introduction to this "universal" consciousness was unexpected and apparently spontaneous. I had never meditated nor taken any mind-expanding drugs. Neither had I read any books describing such an awareness. It was strange in the sense that it was previously unknown to me, but the experience was obviously good and so there was nothing to worry about. After the expanded state of mind had worn off or subsided, I undoubtedly felt changed. I no longer experienced the full intense awareness and non-selfish way of being, although there was a definite residual, left-over effect or memory of this newly-discovered reality.

Other oneness experiences followed in the days and weeks ahead. I am not sure how many or at what intervals because I failed to keep a diary of precise events and dates. They always occurred when I was alone. Each time these experiences seemed to be full and all-embracing. Although I objectively considered the possibility, I knew that I was not going mad.

During these first few weeks, I told someone whom I could trust what was happening. She kindly listened as I used inadequate descriptive expressions like feeling smaller than the smallest ant but larger than the largest mountain - a "tower of power". I explained that each experience afterwards left me feeling purified and transformed, like a butterfly emerging from a chrysalis or pupa. (One of my boyhood interests

14

had been breeding butterflies and moths and studying colonies of ants.)

At this early stage, the process of transformation must have been happening at a quick pace. I can remember one particular incident as a reference point. In the physical time that it took me to leave my room, walk to the bathroom, use the toilet, wash my hands, and return to my room, I underwent not one but three distinct inner transformations. This had all occurred in a matter of a few minutes, clearly indicating an accelerated mental process.

Towards the latter part of September, this mainly solitary period came to an end. I moved to college and soon realised that I had "opened up" as a person much more than I had thought possible. I gradually found a few books which provided some confirmation that others had experienced occasional mystical insights. I also confided in a few close friends. Meanwhile, the oneness experiences continued throughout the next two and a half years. More and more, this expanded state of consciousness became "normal" to me.

One day, all previous insights and awareness came together. A tremendous realisation removed the last mental barrier. I laughed at how slow I had been to see through the final illusion of self. The process of transformation to a different way of being was complete. To me, the enlightenment was staggering - although a close friend who had known me over the previous year or two later commented that it was more like the final dotting of i's and crossing of t's.

I could see with a razor-sharp precision how it was possible for others to gain this same freedom of mind from the pettiness of selfishness. I understood the mechanism of my own awareness and could compare this with that of others around me - resulting in a precise method for seeing what anyone else was doing "right" or "wrong". Everything fitted together in a logical and complete framework. Apparent contradictions of life were easily understood and explained.

I had long before worked out that a mirroring effect took place between myself and others whom I came into contact with in everyday life. This mirroring took many different expressions depending upon the person, but the process was always consistent and logical. I seemed to stimulate people's mental limitations, no matter how normal or mundane the subject of conversation and regardless of the nature of my relationship with them. It was as if my expanded consciousness automatically caused a positive irritation in others. Some people seemed to favourably respond to this, whereas some were defensive or unsure; probably a mixture of both reactions took place in everyone to different degrees. Watching what was happening time after time, I could see that this stimulation always had a potentially positive effect, even if the other person showed outward signs of discomfort. Following full realisation, I used the term "lovingly awkward" to explain this particular interactive effect.

The expanded state of consciousness has constantly stayed with me. It is completely non-selfish in nature, albeit allowing for free-will and individuality. It has ended any suffering caused by dilemma. This new way of being has now been tested by many years of hard experience. I know that it is real, beneficial, and apparently lasting.

3

Clarification

Before continuing with this summarised account of my "personal history", it is important to briefly clarify the nature of these unusual experiences. I wish to minimise any misinterpretations and maximise understanding of these events.

Many others throughout history have experienced mystical revelations. The theme of unity or oneness - of belonging to something greater than the self - is commonly shared. There are different degrees of intensity with such experiences. Sometimes they are seen as being religious or divine in nature. But it is ridiculous to think that all these altered states are merely an aberration of mind. They are certainly not the result of some physical or psychological sickness, like the well-documented paranoia and hallucinations of schizophrenics. So what do they suggest?

What society recognises as the normal self-orientated attitude to life is surely not our full potential. Preoccupation with selfish desires or goals can be powerful and consuming - but it is nonetheless a limited experience. From the day that we are born, there is constant conditioning. This has resulted in a mutual worldwide acceptance of what we consider to be a "normal" state of mind. And yet what I know - initially glimpsed through the ecstatic oneness experiences - is something much more. This expanded state of consciousness not only makes sense of everything that is presently accepted, it goes further. For example, it re-confirms self-preservation as indicated by the natural world and human behaviour - but not exclusively as there is also an insistence on the preservation of the whole.

It is logically consistent that this "universal" consciousness is within the potential of us all. I am sure that it is the next major step forward in our evolutionary path. At present, the human race is limited by its selfishness - but the capacity exists for a greater thinking and wider caring species of man and woman. Education has already stimulated greater flexibility of mind; we have devised amazing technological machines using our expanded mental ingenuity, way beyond the wildest dreams of people who lived just a few hundred years ago. There must be additional scope for this inner development. This is not a matter of belief or speculation; for me it is a constant everyday reality.

Non-selfish consciousness is the full and permanent awakening from the limitations of "normal" con-sciousness. The perception of life or reality is fundamentally different. Perspective and motivation are no longer self-centred; instead, there is only concern for the whole. When the process of change has been completed, it is as if a new species of human being has been born.

There is still much ignorance about altered states of consciousness. The term "enlightenment" is used by many people too easily or loosely; there is confusion about what actually constitutes this radical change. I recognise three levels or stages of transformation. Firstly, there are various degrees and forms of revelation or blissful experience. Secondly, there is the oneness or unity experience in which all selfishness is temporarily left behind. This usually occurs as a "one-off" incident, although it can take place as a repeated event at different times. Afterwards, there is a definite transformation effect. This may be pronounced and it has even been mistaken as "enlightenment" due to the powerful realisation as remembered from the oneness experience. However, subtle forms of selfishness remain or creep back in. The third level or stage produces a constant and completely non-selfish way of being. There is full realisation and appropriate action. This is the real starting point of the new consciousness.

The extraterrestrial contact of 1974 strongly challenged my conditioning and prejudices. It certainly left me changed, The oneness experiences - repeatedly glimpsed during the 1975 to 1978 period - had a sudden, intense, transforming and purging effect on each occasion. But, in between, I was still in what must be called a self-ish state - even though most of my thoughts, feelings, and actions had become altruistic and unselfish. It was only after the final "coming together" in 1978 that I experienced a constant non-selfish consciousness which still remains today.

Clarification

Did the extraterrestrial communication somehow cause the oneness experiences? Was there a connection between these two unusual episodes? The period between September 9th and December 20th 1974 certainly had a profound influence. It brought out a willingness to help and challenged my preconceptions about the world. The period of organising and typing my notes during the summer months of 1975 obviously focused my attention as I searched for rational understanding. This mental process is fully in keeping with the formula I now recognise as leading to an expanded level of consciousness. It is likely that the combination of the effects caused by these and other influential events in my life produced the first ecstasy, which then developed further. They were, at least, of indirect significance. However, in addition to this, it is possible that the initial oneness experiences may have been purposely triggered or "nudged" by the extraterrestrials. The evolution of human consciousness was certainly of interest and concern to them. Whatever the actual explanation, the extraterrestrial incident has to be seen for what it was: a lesser and preceding occurrence. This presumed interplanetary contact was of secondary importance to the very real transformation process which followed.

4

Willing to talk openly and guide

Science has demonstrated that real phenomena are capable of being duplicated under the appropriate conditions. Speculative explanations are formed into a hypothesis which is then repeatedly tested. If the results confirm the hypothesis in an exact and predictable way, this then becomes a theory or working model of reality. I applied the same logical approach of this scientific methodology to my "new" consciousness. I could see every reason why this should also be achievable by others - providing they followed the exact formula to its conclusion.

Everyone at some time feels dissatisfaction with their lives. People suffer "ups" and "downs" and experience dilemma. Non-selfish consciousness offers a permanent release from such inner turmoil. It initially takes effort and practise, but surely the results are more than worthwhile? Knowing this, I spent the first few months after my enlightenment trying to help a number of people who knew about me. Each individual had already started some kind of an inner search for that "something more".

Willing to talk openly and guide

Almost everyone who came to ask questions recognised some benefit during this period. Their awareness was at least more focused. The level of understanding varied with each individual. Most people seemed unclear as to what they really wanted, despite what they initially said. Although I was willing to help and guide, the necessary motivation and effort had to come from the person concerned. Those who showed encouraging signs of progress were always the individuals who conscientiously tried to apply the formula in everyday situations. But there were still those habitual self-limits in the way and few seemed certain about their priorities in life.

Before long, I sensed that this teacher-pupil approach could potentially get out of hand. More people were getting to know about me and a danger lay ahead that the whole situation might be misrepresented by some of those around me. I also felt that the traditional "guru" image was limited in its suitability for the present age and a western country. There had to be a more practical way forward for me to use this consciousness.

In 1979, I announced to everyone who had already come to talk with me that I was going to adopt a different approach. I would willingly co-operate for a further two weeks and then stop answering questions. It was, after all, ultimately their search and responsibility. I had written a short book, published by a group of people around me, so everyone at least had some guidelines on how to proceed. One person in particular, an elderly nun, was progressing at a good pace and would most likely have developed much further with the additional benefit of personal contact. A few people expressed their surprise, but my decision remained and was accepted.

I served people literally for a while, cooking them food in a vegetarian restaurant setting. All the time I continued to explore an alternative approach of stimulating a change of consciousness in others. After this initial experiment, I changed to growing plants having acquired a small piece of land. There were a few instances in which I made an exception to my "keep quiet" approach. For example, a woman from the north of England heard about me from her hairdresser and wrote explaining that she had suddenly experienced a temporary state of oneness whilst walking in the countryside a few years before. It had left her profoundly affected but somewhat perplexed. She travelled south to where I was living and seemed to gain a useful perspective after we had talked for a few hours.

5

Famine in Ethiopia.....
.....to endangered Australian
wallabies

A decision during the 1984/1985 famine in Ethiopia resulted in a spontaneous relief trip to that part of Africa. We went to Makelle in Tigré, one of the worst hit areas, and saw 300,000 starving people. I was deeply moved by what was happening. How could people in the so-called civilized countries have allowed this situation to get so desperate? It was not just poverty - thousands of human beings were unnecessarily dying. We personally distributed the blankets that we had air-lifted, making sure that each one was best used. Much of Ethiopia lies on a high mountainous plateau and the area around Makelle was especially exposed. The bitterly cold nights and lack of shelter at the relief camps often proved too much for the bodies of the weakened famine victims. Our small individual effort helped a few thousand people but seemed totally inadequate for what we saw face to face. We had to do more.

Equally shocking was the general attitude of the aid agencies that we encountered. They seemed largely inefficient and ineffective. By this time, publicity was prompting a massive worldwide response and huge amounts of money had been donated to the charities for the urgently needed relief effort. But where was it? The self-preoccupation and pettiness of the foreign relief workers we encountered - British, Italian, Australian, Japanese and more - was nothing short of appalling. Even when confronted with the horrors of famine, the usual selfishness remained. Most of the people who were supposed to be helping seemed incapable of putting themselves in the shoes of those in desperate need. At the end of the day, it was not their problem. If it had been myself amongst those who were starving and dying, I would have expected someone to help me if they could. Anything less was unacceptable in such a life threatening crisis. Why could people not wake up to this simple truth even in the middle of a major famine?

Dismayed at the typical aid agency attitude that we had encountered, we felt compelled to continue what had only been intended as a "one-off" contribution. Existing plans were cancelled and our efforts directed to helping further. We were back in Ethiopia within a few months, this time with a whole range of relief and development goods for distribution at a famine area in the south of the country. Once more, we saw distressing scenes of severe malnutrition and suffering - all preventable and unnecessary. We also encountered almost unbelievable attitudes amongst many of the foreign aid workers whom we met. A group of Scandinavian nurses, for example, were well looked after by their organisation and each had the luxury of a new vehicle to travel around in - yet they had almost no medical drugs and were typically working just a few hours a day. When we offered to share part of our large supply of 22 basic drugs, they declined to accept the genuine offer.....

The day before returning to England, I travelled north to the Wollo region in a Polish Air Force helicopter and spent several hours at a village on the mountain plateau. A 15-year-old Ethiopian girl died in my arms, weakened by famine and ravaged by illness. I could have almost certainly kept her alive if I had had just a few pence worth of medicine. Trying to feebly comfort the girl's grieving mother and sister, I swore never to forget her.

Shortly before first going to Ethiopia, we had started a conservation project to help endangered wallabies in Australia. These plans now suspended, we formed a second charitable organisation to facilitate our humanitarian work. Attention shifted to Sudan where we entered into a formal agreement with the government authorities to assist in the Suki region. We planned and quickly established an integrated development project to help 3,500 Ethiopian and Eritrean refugees and tens of thousands of local Sudanese villagers. The place at which we were based was flat, featureless and with a hostile environment. A Sudanese military officer told me that his country had two seasons: winter and hell. "Winter" was to us uncomfortably hot, although the nights were chilly. Malaria and a long list of other diseases and disabilities were commonplace.

Practical health care and health education became the main activities of our work, together with income-generating projects - sewing and carpentry workshops and vegetable growing - and general supplementary education for children. We worked non-paid and with a very different approach to that usually taken by international aid agencies. Our policy included obtaining material support whenever practical and we never sought the large budgets used by other organisations. I personally made sure that we always had the appropriate medical drugs and other supplies necessary to carry out the work.

We soon won the respect of the local people and our reputation for consistency spread further afield. The small remote village clinic with its own laboratory was increasingly in demand. Annual numbers of patients examined, diagnosed and treated reached 25,000. The Sudanese authorities were pleased with our efforts, although initially perplexed that we could achieve anything with such a small budget. Occasional visiting foreign aid workers from other organisations often seemed bemused by our approach. A few even openly voiced their surprise at the lack of the usual new land-cruisers and other trappings of aid agency status, yet seemingly failed to notice that we had the only well managed medical drug supply in the area. We quietly continued, involving the local people more and more in our work. The Sudanese and Ethiopian staff were usually quicker to grasp our approach, as we replaced the few British nurses and teachers - perhaps because they more easily identified with the effects of poverty that we were trying to overcome and our simple "no-nonsense" attitude.

In the late 1980s, after gathering extensive first-hand experience at all levels, we carried out an investigation into the inefficiency and ineffectiveness of non-government aid agencies. The field stage of this investigation covered six developing countries in Africa and Asia over a seven and a half month period: Ethiopia, Uganda, Somalia, India, Bangladesh, and Nepal. We interviewed hundreds of field staff (expatriate and local) and visited numerous project sites. The findings were then collated and presented in a confidential report that we circulated to the various organisations and governments. Names were purposely omitted, together with most of the more extreme inadequacies we found. The Sudanese authorities welcomed the report and made sweeping changes in their policies towards foreign aid agencies as a result. There were other positives responses. I am also sure that the report lay gathering dust on several of the aid agencies' shelves, unacted upon - although a number of extra copies were requested by some.

At the end of 1992, we formally handed-over our project work in Sudan to be directed by a highly capable Sudanese woman who continues to take it forward in the same spirit. In 1993, the clinic helped 36,400 patients. We continue to organise an annual shipment of medical supplies that are unavailable in Sudan, but all decisions are now taken by the Sudanese people themselves.

Spending less time organising everything in Sudan, we were gradually able to re-evaluate our ideas to help endangered wildlife. We changed names from The Wallaby Concern to The Wildlife For All Trust and in 1991 at long last formally registered this charitable organisation. We selected a few forgotten or neglected areas - for example, the endangered geometric tortoise and its threatened renosterveld habitat in the south-western Cape, South Africa - but still included our first concern for endangered Australian wallabies. Several overseas field trips and a variety of activities here in Great Britain quickly re-established this commitment to conservation. As we had found with the aid agencies, we soon realised that the claims of certain wildlife organisations were not always what they seemed. Similarities were obvious, especially regarding the ineffective use of much-needed resources. Meanwhile, natural habitat continues to be lost or damaged and unique wildlife faces possible extinction.

6

A combined approach

Since my consciousness changed and the enlighten-ment (or whatever you want to call it) occurred, my only "problem" has been how best to use it for the benefit of others. As you have read, I have personally witnessed the horrors of famine and the lack of development. I have also been touched by the plight of our planet's endangered wildlife and shrinking wilderness. I closely followed the Falklands conflict between our own country and Argentina - and more recently the Gulf War when Saddam Hussein's military forces invaded Kuwait. Murder, rape, and other criminal acts are all around us in our society, together with the more petty squabblings. Knowing this harsh side of life, I remain totally convinced that a solution exists.

A radical change in consciousness towards the non-selfish reality I experience is required. This is the key. It has consistently worked for me and it can have equal benefits for others. As more people awaken to the pitfalls of the selfish approach, the world will also benefit. Survival of the whole is a more logical, practical and complete strategy than the fragmented and short-term objectives of self-preservation on its own.

Although my consciousness is the same as when the final realisation took place, I have gained valuable experience of the outside world during the intervening years. This additional input should be of some use in my aim of helping others to consider and take up this challenge of a greater consciousness and way of being. Recently, I have considered whether it is best to keep quiet about all that I know or to speak more openly concerning these basic issues. Concluding that the latter approach is potentially more advantageous has led to this book being written as one of the first steps in this renewed effort.

Throughout the short time in 1978/1979 when I willingly answered people's questions, I was always concerned about their motivation. Desire for this change of consciousness was serious but often seemed self-centred. With some individuals, the inner searching was compulsive and left little energy to share with the world around them. As the very nature of this desired transformation requires going beyond the limits of self, it was noticeable how much self-preoccupation existed and how little non-selfish action resulted.

So, I am now again willing to answer questions and openly point out the way forward. However, I will strongly urge an appropriate response through unselfish giving. I will firmly insist that if there is to be increased understanding, there must also be increased responsibility - shown in practical action. Anything less than this will be seen as being the product of self-interest or idle speculation. If someone is serious about participating in this transformation process, let them demonstrate their unfolding awareness through some display of self-sacrificing benevolence to the world. When an individual expresses interest to develop, this will be my test: genuine understanding needs to be matched by appropriate outer performance. In the late 1970s, I always suggested this; now, I will only keep talking to someone if such unselfish action actually happens.

7

A blueprint for transformation

Since the "coming together" point in 1978, I have had a fully worked-out blueprint or logical framework which clearly explains what it is I do. Equally, this can be used to assess what others are doing and not doing. The mechanisms of this consciousness are as precise to me as the parts of a motor vehicle are to a mechanic or the components of a television set are to an electrical engineer. I understand it clearly with a sharp exactness. The behaviour of every single person that I have met during the last 16 years or so is logically explainable and predictable according to this framework.

The blueprint is straightforward and practical. The formula is an extension of what is already being done by everybody. Instead of doing some of it, some of the time - it would be better to do more of it, more of the time - or, preferably, all of it, all of the time. There is no gimmick, although parts of the formula are deceptively simple. Objective assessment can be used to plot an individual's progress. If there is some degree of non-understanding or non-application of the formula, a block or limitation point will be noticeable in some way. If needed, I am able to help a co-operative person through any of these stumbling blocks. The formula is testable and suitable for all to do. The practice of it will produce a movement towards a non-selfish, fuller consciousness - in a smoother, more knowledgeable way than the naive "trail blazing" manner of my own transformation.

SECTION TWO:

THE WAY FORWARD

8

Preliminary suggestions

This section is intended as a practical guidebook. It will hopefully add to the inspiration of your inner journey, perhaps motivating and encouraging you to go further forward. It provides suggestions or clues as to the direction and points out a precise way of how to proceed. It outlines the benefits of the journey's end.

Use this main section as a reference book. First understand then try to apply. Read it more than once if you find it helpful. Keep coming back to it. As your consciousness develops, more and more will become clear.

There is always the difficulty of using language. No matter how well the words are selected, they can never fully explain what must be gained by personal experience. This is especially true when describing oneness - a state beyond the so-called normal - and how to achieve it. Careful reading will maximise understanding and minimise misinterpretation. Remember that this is only a book; if you misread it, there is no one to stop you and draw your attention to the error.

9

Normal consciousness:
the life of dilemma

i. Variations

Everyone is uniquely different. Even those who conform
and fit into the stereotyped norm are individually
expressing themselves. Identical twins are different.
No two people are the same. This much is certainly
true.

The common belief of society is that we all experience
more or less the same normal state of consciousness.
Of course, there are variations or degrees as to how we
use this inner ability. Some people are lazy, others
more active. There are tendencies towards or against
the various forms of expression: mental, emotional,
physical - or any combination of these. One person
may be exceptionally intellectually capable or mental-
ly alert; the same individual may be emotionally
restricted or physically unsure. Another person might
be extremely balanced in each form of expression and
with his or her social skills. Whether we describe this
use of consciousness as mundane, average, or
exceptional, the belief is still of the same normal state
of mind available to us all. A minority in society fail to

39

achieve or maintain this more or less normal state of consciousness. We used to call such unfortunate people lunatics; they were mad. More recently, medical science has started to explain these aberrations in terms of psychological sickness (with or without physiological complications).

No matter how talented or ordinary the use or expression might be, we nevertheless recognise these variations as being different points along the same scale of human ability. Such a belief in this normal reality is widely accepted, almost without question.It would appear that we all function within the same range of consciousness.

There is also a general consensus of opinion about the nature of reality. A hundred foreigners visiting California in the USA will all leave with a slightly different impression. Some might have been especially keen to see the showbiz glamour of Hollywood or the fantasy world of Disney. Others might have been captivated by the beach life - including the numerous athletic surfers or attractive, sun-tanned bodies in skimpy swimwear. At least a few visitors will have spent time in California's beautiful wilderness areas, marvelling at some of nature's finest masterpieces. Some will have been impressed by the material goods on offer within the shopping malls of Los Angeles or by the architectural skills that built San Francisco's Golden Gate Bridge. A few will have been uneasy or even terrified by the frequent crime and violence of the big cities. But variations aside, almost everyone would agree upon the same general perception of reality.

There are variations of interpretation. A housewife looks at her table as a solid object. Her scientist husband understands that this apparently solid table is really made up of incredibly minute particles invisible to the naked eye but with an enormous amount of space between them. Their "greenie" son or daughter disapproves that the hardwood timber came from a fast-disappearing tropical rainforest. Some add religious, political, or economic beliefs or considerations to this picture of the world. But each still usually recognises more or less the same picture, no matter how strong the disagreement on the correct interpretation.

ii. The world of desire

You are caught in a world of desire. You always want something. Maybe you really want something badly - or perhaps you are not that bothered, adopting a more laid-back or even apathetic approach to life. Desire might be mild or compulsive, but you still want something.

As a baby, you wanted milk.....then food. You quickly developed a desire for toys. Then you wanted to be liked, so you found friends. As an adult, your world of desire has become a potential endless choice: holidays, cars, babies, television programmes, careers, sport, religion, relationships, etc, etc, etc. Opportunity knocks!

Whether you are a person who is easily pleased or someone who is difficult to satisfy, life is a giant supermarket - a shopping centre! If you are prepared to pay the price, you can have what you want. You have money - you must spend it - you get what you buy. Sometimes you get lucky with a bargain, or you could be fooled into a bad deal. Whatever the degree, the principle is the same. There are shops for everything you can imagine: shops for husbands and wives; shops for material possessions; shops for leisure interests; shops for careers or power; shops to make your body look and feel good; shops to buy salvation and a place in heaven; shops for anything you want - if you are prepared to pay the price.

The world of desire is an endless search for new experiences - mental, emotional, or physical. These experiences might be wildly extravagant or repetitively routine - or anywhere along the same scale. You know no other way. Ignorance of anything better has caused your life to be predictable. There may be patterns and some degree of purpose, but you are still blinded or restricted by your perception of the world. You have discovered the freedom of choice through being alive. You have filled the gap of emptiness in a way suited to your tastes. You may do this intelligently, but it still comes from a limitation of being. There is a lack of deep meaning. What is the purpose of life? Are there complete answers? The treadmill continues as we go around and around, on and on. Even the search for that "something more" - that extra special thing so often just out of reach - comes out of desire. Desire is all you know. In some form of expression, blatant or subtle, to some degree, it motivates and controls you. You are trapped and cannot get out of this endless search! Or maybe you fail to realise this or are not concerned enough to think about it?

iii. The life of "ups" and "downs"

The world of desire results in an endless cycle of "ups" and "downs". Desire has created a mental and emotional state of duality. There is "you" and the "something" you want. When you are getting more or less what you want, you experience positive emotions; when life is going "wrong" - when you are not getting what you want - you experience negative emotions. As before, this process of reaction can be measured or observed to be occurring as variations or degrees along the same scale.

Desire will always bring about disaster - sooner or later, big or small. When life goes "wrong", you become frustrated, worried, annoyed, disappointed, bored, jealous, regretful, bitter, or one of the many other negative conditions. But then life gets "better" - you start to get what you want again - and the negative emotions magically disappear, replaced by positive feelings. Sooner or later, life goes "wrong" yet again and more negative emotions erupt. And so on. The life of "ups" and "downs" is a commonly shared experience; only the variations differ.

You have experienced desire since birth. You choose to continue living it. You are trapped by it. You also have the potential to "pull the plug" on it.....

iv. The strategy of the psychiatrist

The innocence and protected life of early childhood eventually disappears. It might be shattered or may just gradually slip away. The harsh reality of growing up soon dawns. You have to come to terms with the change of this rude awakening. You presume that you are stuck with it and therefore adjust accordingly. Others around you - older, wiser, and more successful than you - have accepted it, so why not do the same? Like any intelligent monkey or parrot, you have learnt to do what others do. You might have copied bits from one person, been influenced here and there by another, picking up the tricks of the game of life as you went along.

Your basic approach to the problem of dilemma has been to minimise the "downs" and maximise the "ups". You have tried to avoid the effects and frequency of the "downs" by limiting - or, if possible, avoiding - any potentially difficult situations that have resulted in negative emotions before. Equally so, you have tried to continue doing the things which produce the "ups". There are variations to this approach - for example, some people get "ups" thriving on negative situations - but the principle is the same.

You have probably never really questioned or discovered if the life of "ups" and "downs" - the world of dilemma - is the only way. It is possible that you have always accepted it as such. Even those who believe or intuitively know that there is a better way, still accept and tolerate the conflicting way of selfishness. Rather than cutting through it, you try to cope with this problematic life. This is the strategy of the psychiatrist.

v. The lie of separateness

You believe in separateness. You accept separateness. You live a life of separateness. Once again, this is true of you all somewhere along the scale - unless you have already realised a state of full consciousness.

You assume that you are the centre of the world - your own part of the world, at least, surrounded by friends and relatives, work and leisure activities, and anything else that you have got from life's supermarket. You adapt to this presumption in an assertive or submissive manner, expressing yourself as an extrovert or, alternatively, as an introvert - or to whatever degree along the scale you choose.

Very simply, you think of yourself as separate and therefore perceive the world around you as a series of separate images. There is "you" and "that out there". Your thoughts, desires, and beliefs are based on or influenced by this idea of separateness. Your actions are an expression or result of it.

You limit your relationship with life. Your thoughts, feelings, and actions are determined by this limitation. You hold back, only going so far. At some point, you are defensive. Your strategy - somewhere along the scale - is to avoid. Intentionally or unintentionally, you do this. You limit your degree of personal responsibility to others and life. At some level - in some form - you turn away.

This idea of separateness comes from ignorance, conditioning, and presumption. It is a lie. You all perpetuate this self-deceit, individually and collectively. It is true that you have a body that is independent from other bodies and that you each uniquely express your individuality - but you are not separate. You have never known actual separateness. Imagined it, yes. Presumed it, yes. Acted on the presumption of it, yes.

The true nature of consciousness is non-separateness or oneness. Consciousness recognises the whole of life in all its forms and expressions. There are degrees of consciousness - but full consciousness goes beyond the limitation of separateness. If you are fully conscious of your real potential, there is no avoidance. There is only a unifying relationship with life. You are a unique, individual expression of this whole - but you are not separate.

Separateness is an illusion which causes a limited state of consciousness. Just because it is presently accepted worldwide as the normal experience does not mean that this assumption is correct. It is not. There is more. We have not yet become properly aware of - we do not use - the full potential of our consciousness. If you believe in separateness, there is a shocking surprise waiting for you to discover. Full consciousness is a reality that can be both glimpsed and/or permanently experienced by anyone.

10

The search for that "something more"

i. Modern myths and stories

There is a greater reality that most people have not yet realised nor discovered. It is possible to glimpse this higher or expanded state before eventually enjoying it on a permanent basis - as I did through the initial oneness ecstasies. Indications of this way forward are contained in various myths and stories. These intimations seem to be updated from time to time. I have chosen three modern examples to illustrate this.

King Arthur and the Knights of the Round Table is a widely known fable. At the beginning of the 1980s, the story was brilliantly told in John Boorman's film *Excalibur*. The theme of unity unfolds from chaotic fighting as a group of brave Knights - guided by Merlin, the magician - defeat the last remaining opposition; the realm becomes one. The Knights promise to form a symbolic round table where they will meet to preserve this hard-won victory. Excalibur is the all-powerful magical sword entrusted to King Arthur to lead the fight for good.

An earlier made film, written and directed by George Lucas, followed by two sequels, portrays the same timeless concepts in a different format. *Star Wars* has become part of our modern culture, with its space-age fantasy appealing to millions of youngsters and adults worldwide. The central hero is Luke Skywalker, a twenty-year-old stuck on his uncle's farm doing dull chores whilst yearning for adventures out amongst the stars. Luke intercepts a cryptic message from a beautiful princess. He then meets the mysterious old man, Ben "Obi-wan" Kenobi, rumoured to have astonishing powers. After his uncle and aunt are brutally killed by stormtroopers of the evil Empire, Luke agrees to learn the ways of a Jedi Knight. Obi-wan teaches Luke how to use an unseen Force that is both around and within us all. Together with a few friends, Luke is catapulted into joining an alliance of freedom fighters who are in the middle of the most savage space-war ever. From this epic trilogy of good against evil came the memorable saying: "May the Force be with you!"

Jonathan Livingston Seagull is an inspirational book by Richard Bach. The story was also made into a movie, with the singer-songwriter Neil Diamond writing the music. It tells of a solitary young seagull called Jonathan who feels that there must be something more to life than just squabbling over scraps of food. He wants to really fly - to go beyond the usual limits. After many early disasters and disappointments, he discovers a few secrets of flight. Convinced that the other seagulls in his flock will be only too eager to hear the good news - and not wanting anything other than to share his newfound freedom of flight - Jon is staggered at the response. He is rejected and made outcast. So begins an inner journey of even greater discovery.....

Six months or so after the oneness experiences had started happening to me, a fellow student at college kindly suggested that I might like to read *Jonathan Livingston Seagull* - commenting that what I was saying sounded similar. This simply told story was the first "outer world" indication I found which seemed to confirm that what I had spontaneously discovered was indeed possible. I have no doubt that this imaginative story has inspired and comforted many others throughout the world in a number of different ways.

ii. Awakening

Most people are surrounded and engulfed by the mist of illusion and limitation. The sensory world of desire - physical or mental - dominates their thoughts and actions. They are not really interested in putting an end to their life of continual "ups" and "downs". They accept the inevitability of mixed happiness and depression from birth to death. Survival of the fittest, in all its complex human forms, is the general rule of existence. There is some mystery to life, but the answers seem beyond reach.

Millions of individuals at some time have had an inclination or intuition that there must be "something more". The feeling or thought may even be strong, almost palpable - but it usually remains elusive and hard to define. Perhaps this instinctive sense is dismissed as idealistic speculation, pushed back into the cupboards of mind and memory. Others turn to religion or some "New Age" alternative philosophy in the attempt to gain some clearer explanation. Many find a physical way to partly express this inner urge for that "something more"; they become artists, sporting enthusiasts, successful businessmen, or choose another path in the hope of gaining a deeper fulfilment.

Those who remain at least partly aware of this unseen potential are awakening. They are willing to make sacrifices and go beyond their limits or what society accepts as the usual norm. The individual is no longer enshrouded in the density of self and begins to desire greater meaning. After this initial recognition or illumination, he or she perceives life as a mystery waiting to be discovered. Slowly, little by little, pieces of the jigsaw puzzle start coming together. The individual has started an inner journey.

iii. The journey

The partly awakened person begins what appears to be a process of unfolding - a quest or search for that "something more". It is a journey of re-discovery - of purification - of eliminating non-essentials - of going beyond the limitations. This journey may take the form of an interest or work pursuit, or it might influence the whole of the person's life activity. At times, it may involve a search through the past - producing a gradual process of re-cognition and re-consideration. It is a quest which brings greater and greater release from suffering, conflict, fear and doubt. The life of dilemma is still there but it is increasingly reduced and seen for what it is.

There is actually no finding of something or reaching somewhere, although it may seem like a finding or reaching. Rather, it is a matter of realising what already is, what has always been and what will always be. There are times of insight and illumination - new beginnings - and also periods of intense suffering and inner desperation. You will repeatedly go through a process of letting go. Dilemma is recognised and faced.

There are usually stops and starts. This is explained very simply. The initial motivation for change may be mixed and not altogether pure. It is often prompted by an outer event which has pushed you so that your back is up against the wall. You are prompted or even spurred into action. There may be initial panic followed by a feeling of exhilaration caused by the release of going beyond. But then complacency sets in, as you experience an increase of comfort or success. You lose the edge. You forget the journey and get caught up in the trappings of adventure. Until further along, when once again you are pushed up against the wall, giving you cause to think again. Beware of the distraction of success or comfort. It will limit and slow you down on the journey to a state of full consciousness.....

iv. Freedom of choice

There are countless possibilities. After taking into consideration our bodily restrictions and that of what we call space and time, nothing is impossible. You can point your life in one direction, or another, or another - any direction you wish. You can choose to use this freedom of choice well or you can choose to use it poorly. You can even choose to let others make the choices for you. You can change your choice at any time and make a new one. You can choose to make the same choice time after time after time - until you get bored or fed up and choose another. You can also choose not to make a choice, convincing yourself that you cannot "because....." - only this is really freedom of choice as well!

v. Hunger

A pupil came to the teacher, seeking to learn. The teacher took him to a nearby river, pushed his head under the water, and held it there for a short time. "When your head was under the water, what did you want most?" asked the teacher. "Air!" replied the pupil. "Come back when you want to learn more than you wanted air!" said the teacher.

If you want something, you must really want it. Nothing is forcing you to want it - but if you do want it, be serious. Go for it! Be hungry!

When you wake up in the morning, you want to put on a clean pair of knickers or pants. You really want to. This early morning routine is a very serious matter. You do it - perhaps nowadays habitually, maybe still half asleep - so you must want to. You have concluded that wearing soiled underwear is neither beneficial nor to be desired. If you carried on wearing the same knickers or pants week after week, month after month, it probably would not kill you - but it would certainly be smelly and unpleasant. Very simply, you put on clean underwear because you want to enough.

Often you want two things at once. For example, perhaps you wish to diet and thereby lose weight. But you also want to eat the same as before, tempted by chocolate or a cake. If the appetite for one is greater than the thirst for another, this fixes the result - unless you choose otherwise. Should you remain indecisive or continue to want both, compromise usually produces half measures.

This principle, like freedom of choice, is important. If you want something a bit, you will usually only get it a bit. If you want it more than anything else, consistently and constantly, you will eventually find a way to get it.

To summarize before going on: remember the possible distraction of comfort and success which can bring about complacency; realise that there is always the freedom of choice; recognise that the focus of your hunger can determine the outcome.

11

The way of *seeing* and *feeling*

i. Knowledge and ability - not belief

Belief is of questionable value. Some people would claim that it provides comfort and a basis for a better way of living. Maybe so. But there is a much more practical and precise way that does not depend upon belief nor faith.

It is what you are and what you do that really matters. Belief, if we are to be totally honest, is of little or no practical value. Believing something does not make us good or bad. What has real effect is the nature of our inner and outer actions. Whatever we choose to do and not do with our freedom of choice has a real effect. How we use our hunger - our wanting - and to what degree this is applied, has a real effect. But belief on its own is little more than belief itself. And it can be a distraction and cause limitation.

At the beginning of this book, I commented that believing what had happened to me was not necessary. I neither asked for belief nor expected it. Why? Because it will not help you. Instead, if you got caught up in the more extreme trappings or manifestations of belief, it could actually hold you back from any possible help. Belief, quite simply, is not very practical.

Disbelief is equally of no value. As with its opposite, it could distract you. Both belief and disbelief - as you may have guessed by now - are merely variations along the same scale. And neither are helpful.

A healthy amount of scepticism is always a good tool to have, providing that it never becomes obsessive and a means to merely disbelieve. Knowing something through verifiable experience and objective examination is the practical alternative to belief. Depending on the subject matter, establishing what is real and what is unreal might be an easy task - or it could require much work through the unravelling of a complex situation.

Your starting point is to realise what you actually know - or think you know - and what you do not know. Make lists if you think this will help to sort out which is which. Then you have to somehow find out what you do not yet know - to make known the unknown. You do this by testing any claim. Look closely at life and see if the idea or claimed truth fits. Examine it not once, but consistently and repetitively. Look for real mechanisms or patterns which are logical and understandable. Search for completeness. Fit together the pieces of a jigsaw puzzle. Be careful not to add any unnecessary presumptions. Be cautious against trying to squeeze something into a place where it really does not belong, even if you would like it to fit. When you are convinced that you really know something is true or real - not through belief but by testing it in the way just described - be open to the possibility that you may still be missing some vital factor or piece of information. Any absent fact could cause a misconception or a partial truth. As a piece of music is made up of precise notes - or a machine by all its components - knowledge is likewise built with exact details.

ii. Preliminary skills

So far, we have examined the nature of normal consciousness and the structures of our conditioning. Next, we established a few specific principles. Now, I will draw attention to four preliminary skills you will need. Develop and fine tune them. This is important.

The first preliminary skill required is a receptive alertness. A lazy or apathetic mind will hinder you. Equally so, too fast a mind that runs ahead of complete understanding is an imbalance. A closed mind will merely block. So you need to be actively-passive or passively-active. Be aware of your preconceptions and prejudices as these will distort. Mental agility and a watchful disposition will be of great use. Be critical without criticising for its own sake. Be open-minded and yet definite. Be ready to learn from anything and everything. Cultivate this capacity for receptive alertness.

The second ability is concentration. Lazy-mindedness will impede your progress. A distracted or butterfly mind will wander from the path, leaving you tangled and lost. Learn to centre or focus your perception and reasoning. You must be able to intensify this concentrated attention whenever you want. The mental control should be flexible and fluid. Polish this aptitude until it comes naturally and easily.

The third qualifying expertise is best expressed using the immortal words of William Shakespeare: "To thine own self, be true." You cannot be whatever your relatives or friends think you should be. Some people, unfortunately, want you to conform to this way or that way. They expect you to be something you are not - nor wish to become. If you submit to this subtle type of blackmail, you will become fragmented or two-faced. If you care for others and yourself, the only solution is to do your best as much as you can. Doing what you really want to do, trying to live up to the highest standards you think are most excellent, is all that anyone should or could expect. Nobody can ask more. You cannot live someone else's life for them - and they cannot live your life. By being true to yourself, you are being true to others in the deepest sense. Superficiality and game-playing will inhibit you. Take personal responsibility for your own way of being. To thine own self, be true!

The fourth preliminary skill you require is the ability to act now. There is only now. And now. And now. The future starts now. And now. And now. Awareness can grow now. Freedom of choice is an opportunity that is available now. And now. And now.

iii. The activity of *seeing*

> *The trouble with most people is that they will*
> *not listen to what the trouble with them is.....!*

Seeing is the activity of enquiry. You need to probe and consider - make an investigation - examine and search for knowledge - scrutinise. You should consciously enquire whenever something new arises.

Enquiry occurs as a question. This question can take any form. Perhaps one of the simplest is to ask: "Is this true?" or "Is this real?" Other useful expressions include: "What causes my dilemma?" - "Am I holding back, limiting my involvement - and, if so, why?" - "When does separateness occur?" - "What am I doing?" - "How can I do more?" - "Am I avoiding a fullness of relationship?" A few preliminary forms of enquiry that should be asked are: "Am I using my freedom of choice appropriately?" - "What do I really want?" - "Do I want realisation more than anything else?" - "Do I want to go beyond all of my petty limitations?" - "Am I content to believe or do I really know?" - "Am I being receptively alert - actively-passive?" - "Do I get distracted?" - "Am I focused?" - "Am I true to myself?" - "Am I doing my best?" - "Am I concerned with now?"

Seeing can occur as an inner or outer enquiry. Your examination must be honest and as objective as possible. Your motivation must be to rise above the delusions and restrictions of self as you know it. You have to really want to find the answer - the complete answer. *Seeing* reaches out, not in a blind or erratic manner, always penetrating the veils of ignorance. It is crucial that enquiry occurs as a real question that must be answered - not just as an intellectual or philosophical exercise. It is concerned with removing the barriers of illusion, limitation, and separateness.

If you are going to find any part of this precise and practical formula difficult to comprehend, it will probably be *seeing*. It may seem like an elusive ability, remaining just out of reach. The concept is easy to generally understand - but a more exact grasp might be obscure and intangible. Therefore, you should think of *seeing* as the way to expose selfishness. Enquiry or questioning is the means to challenge the thoughts and actions of selfishness. First stop yourself, then confront and investigate what you are doing. The task is to detect and lay bare the egotistical or self-interested habits that you have been conditioned into accepting as normal. *Seeing* can reveal these complex and subtle tendencies - allowing you to dismantle the attach-ments to this "normal" pattern of being and open up to a wider consciousness.

Seeing is vitally important. Do not underestimate its power or scope. Use it internally and externally. It is the way to overcome what holds you back.

iv. The experience and effect of *seeing*

Once awake to the possibility of that "something more", *seeing* stimulates and allows a correction from the life of dilemma towards a greater consciousness and way of being. The thoughts, desires, and actions begin to change. The grip of selfishness starts to loosen.

Enquiry sooner or later leads to a partial or complete understanding. This increases awareness. Your perception is altered by the insight. There is a re-cognition - a letting go of some limiting thought, belief, or desire. At times, *seeing* might be experienced as a kind of dying to the old way of being - a re-birth into a new world. It could be felt as a relief or release. There is a clearer appreciation of life.

Seeing should take place whenever there is confusion or dilemma. To begin with, this might occur after the upset has happened. Gradually, it becomes possible to exercise the process of enquiry as the disruption is being experienced - thereby reducing or even stopping the emotional imbalance. At other times, *seeing* should precede any dilemma - possibly averting it. Use *seeing* when you are in a stable mental state or to bring about a greater clarity of mind.

The effect of *seeing* is transformation. It can be experienced as a series of degrees along the same scale. You recognise first the fact and then the nature and activity of the situation. You become increasingly aware of patterns and mechanisms that have been developed through years of conditioning and selfish reaction to life. There is the perception of order within apparent chaos. There is good where you previously saw only bad - hope within despair - light at the end of the tunnel. On occasions, it might feel like a metamorphosis. There could be a radical change of awareness or a slight alteration, depending upon the situation or extent of ignorance requiring penetration. Understanding replaces confusion. It involves a realisation which illuminates the inter-relatedness of life. There is a shift towards appreciation of the whole.

v. *Feeling* - a fullness of relationship

The lie of separateness is at times experienced as an inner contraction. You withdraw or hold back. Dilemma, confusion, and ignorance cause this contraction. Your consciousness is restricted. You are confined by the narrowness of mind or by the weakness of spirit.

Seeing - as we have just examined - is the way to pierce the bubble of illusion and delusion. We start to understand as awareness grows. The effect is a degree of transformation. With this increased consciousness comes a greater sense of involvement or *feeling*. There is an opening up of the heart, which is no longer denied, detached, or locked away.

As before, *feeling* can be experienced as a series of points along the same scale. However, the potential for total *feeling* - like the unlimited capacity for a complete understanding of *seeing* - is always there, waiting to be used within you. It is a wholeness of concern.

Feeling can be described as an all-powerful love or caring. It is unlimited, never-ending, non-dependent.

It is a breakdown of the meanness of self. It is a non-selfish giving. It flows as effortlessly as the water in a stream or river moves towards the sea - sometimes gushing as a torrent, sometimes gliding smoothly, occasionally waiting. It is a celebration of life through expression. It is a purity of passion.

Feeling is a fullness of relationship. There is non-selfish involvement. The intense completeness is absolute. It is impossible to turn away or to deny. There is no opposition - only oneness. You can only answer: "Yes, I will." The twisted emotions and impurities of selfishness are washed away. What remains is a caring for the whole. The heart is open.

vi. Heart and mind - working together

The way of *seeing* and *feeling* is a process of becoming and being. It is an absolute way. The journey towards this totality of being takes place along a scale. There are degrees of experience or revelation - although in truth there is only absoluteness. There is a dream state of part truth, part illusion. You know this as your everyday normal reality. But as awakening occurs and the gift of life unfolds, the dream begins to slip away.

The way of *seeing* and *feeling* is the correct use of both mind and heart. It is the true state of verbal and non-verbal communication. The mind clears the way for the heart. The heart fills the body. There is no more confusion. There is no more emptiness. Enlightenment or full realisation is the permanently expanded state of this process - the ability to constantly function at the most open point of the scale. There is the uncluttered capacity to understand and care.

The more you *see* - the more you *feel*. If you think this is not happening, you are failing to recognise some crucial blockage - so enquire! *Seeing* and *feeling* are intrinsically related.

The mind without the heart is a cold and sterile place. There is only intellectualisation. The heart adds warmth and meaning. It is essential that you understand this inter-relatedness of function. You need to master both *seeing* and *feeling*. Using one without the other is an imbalance which should be corrected.

12

The "spinning-top" effect

i. Bursting the bubble

You are hopefully understanding that it is possible to overcome the suffering of dilemma. By re-reading certain pages, such as the previous part about *seeing* and *feeling,* your understanding should increase. But quietly reading a book is a long way from applying the formula throughout the whole of your everyday life. You now need to sharpen the preliminary skills and apply the principles in each and every situation - both inwardly and outwardly. You have to start practising.

Jumping ahead, there is a major difficulty to overcome. How can you penetrate the lie of separateness when everything you think, want, and do is either based upon or influenced by it? How can you burst the final bubble that holds you back?

> *The teacher remarked to the pupil: "Your problem is that you are seeing double." "Impossible!" replied the pupil. "If that were so, there would be four suns in the sky instead of two!"*

To free yourself from the lie of separateness - the life of selfishness and dilemma - you first must be prepared to go beyond yourself. You need to have the enthusiasm and daring of an adventurer. Eventually, a point will come when you find yourself at the edge. You will have to jump off this edge with no chance of recovery. You need to "kill" the limiting self-image and defensiveness which you think of as your "self". The image of separateness that you have been conditioned into believing must die. You might try to cling on to it - or be unsure of how to overcome it - possibly thinking that the alternative is oblivion and loss of identity. Before you reach this critical decision, it is likely that you will have to face similar inner tests of resolve at earlier points of the journey.

Conditioning is not easy to overcome - but it can be done. The habitual bonds have to be disentangled and the knots untied. If you want this - really want this - go for it! Any Olympic gold medallist will tell you that the special feeling of reaching that ultimate goal is worth all the training, early disappointments, and sacrifice.

ii. From effort to effortless

Millions of people now successfully operate computer software programmes as part of their daily work routine. At first, the new technology was strange and looked complicated. There was hesitation and a reluctance to change. When youngsters quickly took up the challenge and became skilful, many older people grew even more apprehensive. Feelings of mild inadequacy were complicated with the fear of failure, embarrassment, and possible ridicule. But increasing numbers of adults have successfully re-trained and now manage to competently use this new computer potential. Nobody learnt it overnight. People have had to read and re-read the reference books or attend tuition courses. And they have had to practise and practise. When mistakes were made, countless beginners no doubt cursed the computer - only to find that the fault lay with human error. When it was the operator's fault, this took some getting used to. Outsmarted by a machine! Only because the system had been set up in a logical and precise way. Most operators never bother to exploit the full potential of their computer software programmes; they usually choose to stop learning as soon as they are reasonably proficient, enabling them to do their jobs properly. With further practise, the new skills they have acquired become easy to use at last.

There are a number of parallels between the above example and the subject of expanding your overall consciousness. You have to overcome the initial strangeness, want to do it, be reasonably open, con-centrate, etc. It requires effort. And there is a level at which you might become complacent and stop learning, at least temporarily. But with practise, anyone can learn how to do it and be successful.

Once you have reached a certain point, if you want complete transformation, *seeing* and *feeling* must be intensified and extended to everything that limits a fullness of relationship with life. There can be no exception - no stone unturned. If you are able to do this to its logical conclusion - not briefly, but constantly - the effort that you will have needed will then be replaced by an effortless mechanism through the completeness of *seeing* and *feeling*.

Imagine a child's spinning-top - a toy which you have to repeatedly push a knob or handle downwards to make the spinning-top go around. You have to push and push and push and push, but eventually (if and when you have pushed hard and quickly enough) the spinning-top spins around on its own; you then sit back and watch it. What I am describing is similar to this, with the exception that there is a certain point which, if reached, causes the inner spinning-top effect to carry on and on without slowing down again.

It is easy to overlook that which holds you back. What you do in the false belief of separateness is very normal to you. You have known no other way. It goes unchallenged and unquestioned. There are habitual reactions that you accept without thinking. These subtleties of mind must be sought out and exposed with the illumination of enquiry and understanding. There can be no room for complacency.

A skilled artist travelled far to find the master. "Please will you teach me more?" he asked. "Certainly" replied the master. "Draw this small bird and wait for me to return."

Very soon, the artist had sketched an exquisite picture of the bird. Thinking that the master would be pleased with his fine work, he was content. Half an hour passed and the pupil became impatient. After an hour, the master had still not come back. Irritated, the pupil went to find him. "Go back and wait for my return as I instructed!" was the only thing the master would say. Even more frustrated and somewhat annoyed, the artist did as he was told.

Another hour went by and the master remained elsewhere. Gradually, indignation turned to boredom. Then the pupil-artist cast his eye back to the bird. Looking at it anew, he noticed the bird's delicate feathers and again started to draw. He produced sketch after sketch, each a study of exact detail. Hour after hour, he drew the bird's various feathers, its eyes, and feet. When the master finally returned, he was pleased.

If there is any contraction or holding back, there must be more for you to *see* and unblock. A fullness of consciousness and relationship with life will only happen when there are no more inhibiting limitations. This is the simple test of whether you have done enough. If not, continue with the task of applying the way of *seeing* and *feeling*. Renew your resolve with a freshness of mind and spirit.

iii. Slow or fast?

In the early stages of the journey, you may choose to go slowly or fast. The decision of pace is yours to make as you wish and at this stage is not critical. What really matters is that awakening dawns and the preliminary skills are acquired. Progress is progress. Everyone's path is uniquely different, even if the principles that need to be learnt and applied are precisely the same.

The "spinning - top" effect

There are usually distractions and dead-end turnings to begin with. These may not at first be recognised as such, perhaps offering something attractive or comfortable. But they will delay progress through diverting attention from the real issue. Whatever happens, lessons are always around to show you the way. A degree of ignorance will usually lead to some blind alley. Experience is necessary for you to learn. Accept all episodes in your life as opportunities. Every occurrence - whether it seems negative or positive - is a potential signpost to freedom.

Truth can be a difficult thing to grasp. Sometimes it is so simple that we have to unlearn before we can understand. Truth or knowledge can also be complex with many intricacies and angles to consider, as the following illustration shows:

> *A man is walking up a mountain from the south side; he looks up and is sure that the summit lies to the north. A second climber approaches from the north; he looks up and is equally certain that the mountain top lies to the south. Two other climbers are ascending from the east and west directions; they would each respectively swear that the summit is to the west and east. In reality, the mountain remains in the same place. It is the perspective of the climbers from whatever point they are at which causes the apparent discrepancies. When the top is reached, they all share the same view.*

A consistent attitude and approach is required towards the end of the journey. To fully penetrate the lie of separateness, you need to remove every last obstructive limitation. Imagine yourself floating in space, imprisoned by a brick-built room. You will only be free once every last brick has been knocked out. But there is a problem. If you stop, the bricks come magically floating back into place. Should this happen, you have to push them out again. Consistent effort is most certainly necessary until effortless freedom finally arrives. Be very aware of this when applying the way of *seeing* and *feeling*. To whatever degree you want to succeed, it must always come first in your list of wants.

iv. Forgetfulness and excuses

Two of the most persistent enemies which stand in the way of progress are forgetfulness and the excuses of limitation.

Gaining awareness requires effort, but forgetfulness is ever-present to pull you back into the dream-world that you think of as reality. It might therefore be helpful to use some kind of a reminder, but without becoming dependent upon it as a crutch rather than a tool. Forgetfulness begins almost immediately after awareness, so be careful and keep yourself receptive and alert to this possibility. Re-reading this book will help as a reminder.

The excuses of limitation can at times be both powerful and irrational. The prospect of opening up or going beyond seems to often cause a problem. Defensiveness takes over and some find themselves saying: "I can't because....." So be it! That is their freedom of choice. Unawareness or forgetfulness has clouded their minds and kept their hearts closed. With some people, you can try helping them but they do not want to know. They even perhaps start arguing for their limitations as if these constraints were some cherished possession! To quote the old saying: "You can lead a horse to water, but you cannot make it drink." The excuses of limitation can be very subtle. Watch out and expose them for what they are: an illogical strategy which will only hinder your development and potential.

13

The way of surrender

i. Letting go

If you want something enough, you have to reach out and grab it. Then, if you change your mind, you have to let go of the first thing in your hand to make room for the next object of desire. You usually employ this process of letting go after losing interest in what was previously treasured or perhaps when it no longer serves your purpose. This is true whether it involves another person, an idea, or a material possession. Like the other principles of the formula I am describing, you already know how to do this to some degree or in some situations - somewhere along the scale.

We have already established that you need to let go all the limitations that hold you back. You do this by following the way of *seeing* and *feeling*. If something is of no use to you, drop it. Throw it out! Do you keep your kitchen garbage or other rubbish inside your house, month after month? No, of course not. You get rid of it. You let it go. Why keep it? If you did, the house would start to smell! Letting go of your inner rubbish is no different. The enquiry of *seeing* allows you to identify what to let go of. Ask yourself: "Is this rubbish?" Ask the question: "What will happen if I keep this?" Much of what you hold on to is garbage. You have been conditioned into becoming a collector of trash! You accept this as normal because everyone does it. Would you wipe your dirty bum with your hand? No? Millions of people in the developing countries do this using their left hand as a normal everyday habit. We in the so-called developed countries choose to use toilet paper instead because it is more hygienic and less unpleasant. We have the choice. Just because one way is considered normal does not mean that it cannot be dropped for another way which is preferable.

Different people are attached to all kinds of limiting rubbish. There is attachment to the physical body. You may be addicted to some bodily desire. For example, I have seen many people here in England get upset if they did not receive their regular meals on time for some reason. Could they abstain from eating for 24 hours without their minds being filled with anguished thoughts of food? Yet in other cultures, fasting is considered to be a normal discipline that is willingly carried out at certain times. The dieting industry thrives and gets rich exploiting this bodily attachment to the excessive eating of food. I once sent an article to a dieting magazine about famine in Ethiopia - but they declined to publish it. Maybe they were worried it might shock some of their readers out of their petty inadequacies - thereby losing the company valuable income? (Their advertising customers selling other diet industry products would hardly have been pleased to see such an article included in the magazine either!) Perhaps they were more attached to the desire of selling large numbers of the periodical than genuinely interested in helping people overcome their addiction and weakness?

There is attachment to ideas. How many discussions about religion or politics have you heard that ended in a blazing argument? And memories. Have you ever misplaced your keys and spent ages looking for them in a certain place - getting annoyed that you could not locate them - only to then remember or find out that you left them elsewhere? Or possibly you are haunted by the memory of some traumatic event? And physical possessions. And other people. And careers. How many people are bored with what they do but fail to let go and make a change - paralysed by the fear of insecurity - unless they have already found an alternative job to switch to?

You are attached to many things. The past may have a hold on you. Or you might choose to avoid the now by dreaming of the future. You are probably attached to some of the normally accepted social values, unable to go against them - perhaps to do with family relations. Or you might have replaced them with a more outrageous set of alternative social values - thinking that you are different and free - when really you have merely joined a sub-culture of society. A few people are attached to solitude.

If you are attached to something, you will probably defend it. You could use ignorance as your defence or passionately justify your choice of action with thought-out reason. Either way, you need to let go. Dump the rubbish.

You are holding back or holding on. If you want everything, it is impossible to cling on to something. Open your hand.

ii. Appropriateness and preferences

If there is no attachment or dependency, what is left? Nothing? Does a woman with beautiful long hair have to cut it off or cover it up by becoming a nun? Can we enjoy anything? Do we have to live a life of emptiness and deprivation? No.

We can do anything - enjoy anything - so long as it is appropriate. Forget what society calls "right" or "wrong" as this tends to change with each country and age. Rely on the way of *seeing* and *feeling*. Do your best to understand. Open up your heart. Be true to yourself. This will show you what is appropriate.

It is not appropriate to kill another human being if you have penetrated the lie of separateness and experienced the oneness of a greater consciousness. But it might be appropriate if this other human being imminently threatens to kill your wife or child and there is no other defensive way to stop this happening. It might be inappropriate to do nothing, especially as the attacker is himself acting inappropriately. Regardless of which decision you take, someone will be killed - so is it not more appropriate to intervene and save the innocent person? Wars should be unnecessary and inappropriate. But unfortunately they still occur out of man's inhumanity to man. People get killed, usually including those who never wanted the war and

Human Potential

rarely the few that started it. Property gets destroyed.
If we are faced with a man like Hitler, it is appropriate
to stop him and his armies - even if we are forced to go
to war ourselves. To do nothing would be inappropriate
if we believed in freedom and cared for what happened
to the Jewish people who were being butchered. And if
we care more for the taste of meat than we do for the
right of animals to live, it is appropriate to eat meat.
However, if we care more for the life of the animals
than we like eating their flesh, it will then become
appropriate for us to be vegetarians. Everything is
based on what you *see* and *feel*.

Where there are choices between different appropriate
actions, this is resolved through preference.
Sometimes this can be decided on the degree of
appropriateness - which is the action that has a
greater appropriateness. In situations where this
seems to be unnecessary, individual preference should
be exercised. For example, eating food which is
poisonous would be obviously inappropriate if you
wanted to stay alive; eating food which is less fattening
would be more appropriate than consuming another
food with a higher calorific value if your choice was to
lose weight; choosing between different makes or
flavours of ice-cream would be a matter of individual
preference, based on experience.

Compulsive desire is therefore unnecessary. Selection
based on appropriateness and preference is compatible
with the way of *seeing* and *feeling*. It allows action and
enjoyment. It does not restrict spontaneity nor a
healthy appetite for life. You do not have to become
some "other-worldly" saint-like figure. If you disagree

76

with something, you can express your disagreement - calmly or with strong passion, depending on the situation. You can live a full and active life.

iii. Non-selfish action

The way of *seeing* and *feeling* provides the clarity and understanding of the mind together with the purity and openness of heart. The way of surrender is a way of action. It calls for a fullness of responsibility and relationship. It recognises total involvement, now. The love and caring of oneness must be shared.

Normal consciousness produces an inclination towards self-orientated action. There is an emphasis on first looking after one's self. With age, this limited centre of concern usually expands to include immediate family members and perhaps a few close friends. Occasionally, there may be exceptional acts of unselfish behaviour.

Seeing and *feeling* generates a different importance. As the grip of self-preoccupation is gradually loosened, there must be a re-orientation towards more non-selfish action. Prominence is placed on caring for and helping others, as well as yourself. Realisation unfolds that it is the whole that matters, not just the part. Individual preferences are balanced and re-adjusted, with increased surrender of your life to the needs of the whole. You not only cease to add to the world's problems, you also consciously and actively contribute to the solution. Non-selfish service is the test of whether progress towards full consciousness is real.

When the formula is fully applied, there is freedom from the limitations of separateness. There is no more selfishness. It becomes impossible to turn away from the whole. Therefore, in a way, there is also a loss of freedom. Personal sacrifice becomes normal. This realisation of oneness includes yourself - and there should always be some time allocated for your individual interests, even if you choose to greatly reduce these. Concern for your own passions is seen against the wider context of what is needed for the benefit of all. Giving has become more important than taking or receiving. There is a laying down of everything that is selfish. This is the way of surrender.

14

A summary

I have purposely tried to keep my words simple. Rather than write hundreds of pages, I elected for a concise and straight-to-the-point approach. It is therefore important that each paragraph should be carefully considered and understood as much as possible. At all times, I have attempted to de-mystify the subject. I have concentrated on the here and now. There is no philosophy nor speculation in my words - only the description of a precise formula that is totally practical. It is based on my own transformation. By following the formula, you will expand your consciousness outwards from the limitations of selfishness.

This "how to" summary is included as a quick-glance reference or reminder. So, once again - this time in abbreviated format - here is what you need to do:

■ Be aware that normal consciousness is not full consciousness.

■ Remember that you always have freedom of choice.

■ Realise that if you want something, you need to really want it.

■ Understand that it is ability which is important, not belief.

■ Acquire the preliminary skills of receptive alertness and concentration. Always be true to yourself. Act now.

■ *Seeing* begins with a question that needs an answer. Understanding follows this initial process of enquiry.

■ *Seeing* allows greater *feeling* - a fullness of relationship and caring.

■ Heart and mind must work together.

■ You have to burst the bubble that is the lie of separateness.

■ There must be consistent effort.

■ Remember that forgetfulness, excuses, and complacency threaten to inhibit your progress.

■ Let go all that restricts you.

■ Appropriate action and the selection of preferences provide an alternative to compulsive desire.

■ Service through non-selfish action is required. Avoidance is replaced by involvement.

If you get stuck, you must be missing something. Keep asking what. Go back and read everything again - this time more carefully and precisely.

15

Crisis? What crisis?

i. Is life on Earth getting better or worse?

If we were visited by intelligent beings from another
planet, how would they see life on Earth today? Would
these extraterrestrials see the human race as
civilized, barbaric, or a mixture of both? What would
they think of us? The answers, of course, would
depend upon a number of factors: the degree of their
own understanding and development of consciousness;
their familiarity with the intricacies of our various
cultures; how much they had studied us through
precise observations over a period of time. However, it
would certainly be interesting to get an "outside"
opinion or perspective. Such an independent
assessment could be very useful as a means to shake
us out of our limited and habitual ways of looking at
life. But would we be reluctant to hear or accept some
of what could be said to us? If we are to believe *Star
Trek*, the fictional television series, there may perhaps
be some kind of galactic agreement whereby extraterrestrials are obliged to limit the degree of their
interaction with - and influence upon - less advanced
planetary races. If this were so, the term "less
advanced" would probably include ourselves; after all,
our off-planet travelling has only recently begun and

is still in its infancy. Extraterrestrials or not, we can take a hard look at life on Earth for ourselves.....

As we head closer to the year 2000 A.D., people are still fighting wars. Many of these outbreaks of mass fighting take place as civil wars or regional clashes within the boundaries of a single country. Others commonly take the form of cross-border skirmishes or on-going territorial disputes. Occasionally, a major international war breaks out. Armed conflict and hostilities have not yet been relegated to the history books. Some countries are still prepared to use military aggression against their neighbours to secure what they want. If they think it is possible to get away with using such tactics, these countries are willing to strike first. This usually forces a response with the aim of defence or achieving international peace and fairness. Most disputes are complicated by historical, political, economical, and possibly religious factors. But they are still happening, year after year.

There are small groups of terrorists who are prepared to inflict suffering on others in the hope of achieving some political goal. They are willing to kill innocent passengers aboard aircraft, including women and children, to achieve publicity and leverage. Others take foreign hostages, often with the aim of striking a bargain that will suit their objectives. A few restrict their terrorism to damaging property. In each case, these fanatics or extremists are exercising their freedom of choice in a way that overrules or takes away the freedom of other individuals. The terrorists justify this behaviour in the name of their cause. The views and intentions of the victims are seen as being of a lesser worth or consequence than their own political agenda.

Cold-blooded murder is an everyday occurrence somewhere on our planet. The numbers show this is not an occasional happening. The motive for the heartless killing is always a form of selfish greed, whether those murdered are selected targets or innocent bystanders. Other murders or manslaughter deaths result from the uncontrolled emotional disputes between friends and relatives. In all cases, life is prematurely taken away. Usually, this has a devastating effect upon those who remain and were close to the person killed.

Rape is another horrific atrocity that plagues our world. The sickness of self-preoccupation combined with a blatant disregard of others even allows some rapists to attack children. Lives are shattered by such intimate assaults - memories frequently haunting and influencing the victims long after the offence took place.

Other crimes testify to man's continued inhumanity to man. Stealing is justified by the thief on the grounds that someone else has what he or she wants, somehow making this action acceptable. We hear that unemployment is to blame - not selfishness?! There is often a degree of organisation in crime, especially where large amounts of money are involved, such as with the trade in narcotics. There is a constant struggle between the efforts of international law enforcement agencies and the powerful crime syndicates.

Young people turn to drugs in apparently increasing numbers, disillusioned by what society can offer or tempted by those around them. Heroine and glue-sniffing severely distort reality; addiction to such dangerous substances damages outlook and health - and can even kill. Abuse of alcohol likewise ruins the lives of many. We now know that smoking tobacco can severely damage an unborn baby - yet there are plenty of pregnant women and their partners who are still selfishly unwilling to change or suspend this habit.

People continue to die on our planet because at times their crops repeatedly fail and there is not enough food. They begin to starve and their weakened bodies become more susceptible to illness. Not only is there unnecessary death on a large scale during these times of famine, prolonged suffering or permanent disfigurement is a widespread and continuous daily event in many developing countries where basic medical facilities are scarce or beyond the reach of the poorest. Tiny amounts of money, if used correctly, can mean the difference between life and death or health and disability. This is more than just poverty. Whatever we want to call it, such neglect is needless, intolerable, and obscene. As a planet, we have more than enough. In comparison to the poorest who fail to survive or are crippled for life, every person living in a so-called developed country is a millionaire. There is so much information available today about our world that we no longer have any excuse for this utter disregard and selfishness. If there is still ignorance, it is the ignorance of choosing not to think and choosing not to care. Countries like Ethiopia and Sudan are not on some distant planet where it is difficult or impossible to reach; it takes only a few hours by air to travel to these countries. If properly organised, it would be possible to drastically reduce much of the painful suffering and death that still goes on and on.

Animals suffer exploitation in numerous ways, revealing our barbaric and hypocritical attitudes. We share the same planet with these creatures and so have a right to interact with them. It is even appropriate that we manipulate their activities in certain ways where there is some benefit. For example, scaring birds away from airport runways is a sensible manipulative action to prevent them flying into aeroplanes, thereby averting death to them and possible damage to the aircraft. Animals often adapt to human enterprise in ways that are advantageous, making use of any helpful modification to their environment. What matters is acknowledging the principle of the right to co-exist. But instead, mass cruelty continues. For example, human beings kill certain wild animals because of wanting to wear their attractive furs and skins. Are people freezing to death with no other option? No, it is simply freedom of choice and thinking only of yourself; the person wants to look good through wearing a fur coat. Society tolerates a huge amount of exploitation of animals - wild and domestic - causing their pre-mature death and unacceptable levels of suffering on a massive scale. What right have people to kill a lamb - to take away its life - just because they want to eat it? Are they starving? Is it necessary? No, it is merely the freedom of choice acting out of greed. You like the taste of the meat more than you like the lamb living and expressing itself. You pay people to breed and farm sheep and other livestock, to slaughter them, then to chop up and package the meat on your behalf. Yet millions of vegetarians worldwide live a normal healthy existence on a diet which does not involve the killing of intelligent creatures - and they still enjoy their meals. Does dominance really give humans the right to kill for greed and pleasure? If so, would you apply the same thinking that advanced extraterrestrials - who could perhaps dominate us if they chose - thereby have the right to eat us? Surely there must be a principle of maximum co-existence?

In addition to the subject of animal welfare, there is also the question of exploiting our natural resources. Have we the right to change the face of planet Earth so much that we unnaturally force unique species of the animal and plant kingdoms to extinction? Four Australian wallabies are already presumed to be extinct, for example, as a result of man's interference with nature since the 1800s. Many more of these beautiful marsupials are currently endangered or vulnerable. Countless other species throughout the world face an uncertain future. We are destroying or damaging their habitats. We are polluting the rivers, lakes, seas, and air around us. People are becoming increasingly aware of these environmental problems, but are we all doing enough? Extinction is irreversible. Once a species is gone, it is lost forever and our planet becomes a poorer place.

Neither should we forget the mass internal confusion and misery. How many people become so depressed that they temporarily give up and have what we call nervous breakdowns? How many others come close to this at times? Some actually commit suicide in their desperation. Others make a half-hearted attempt or threat, crying out for someone to help and care. There is intolerance and bigotry. There is exploitation and persecution. Many seek power at the expense of others. If someone gets in the way, tough! Many prefer to keep themselves to themselves and shut out the world whenever possible. Survival of the fittest - evident in animals - still applies. People learn all kinds of ways to get ahead and stay ahead - or, at least, remain safe in their own little cocoons. The pettiness of selfishness and the hurt it causes is perpetuated throughout the human race. This is more or less accepted as normal or inevitable and thereby condoned.

The problems are enormous and the tidal wave of selfishness is undeniably strong. To make matters worse, the human population is growing at a disturbing rate. More people will mean less space to go around. More resources will be needed to sustain the increased population even at a subsistence level. Meanwhile, there is emergency after emergency that requires our immediate aid and attention. Are we gradually heading for a major worldwide crisis? Is this alarmist? Is there any hope?

The other side of human nature offers optimism. There are clear signs of an ability to go forward, to overcome the many hurdles of life, to find something special within the mundane. At its best, the individual human mind and spirit can be a remarkable and wonderful expression of life. This is not just an isolated one-in-a-million freak accident of nature - it is readily observable all around us in varying degrees.

We all recognise the talent and determination of individual and team-orientated sports men and women. There are countless examples of those who achieve a high standard of excellence in their chosen event. We see it on a worldwide scale during the summer and winter Olympic Games - and throughout the other major international championships and competitions. Each person who achieves this physical excellence has also had to use their mental qualities. Whether knowingly or not, they have developed much of the inner ability which I have described within this book to a surprisingly high degree. The main difference is that they have channelled these skills as a means to advance their sporting aspirations, rather than learning to use and apply them in a wider and more complete sense.

Thousands of known examples testify to the bravery and unselfishness displayed by man. Both in times of war and peace, individuals have exposed themselves to great risk to help or save another whose life was threatened. Others have equally put themselves in jeopardy for the sake of saving an endangered animal or in the name of a different but equally worthy cause. Whatever the purity of motive, the signs of sacrifice are clear. And if it is possible to go beyond the pull and limitations of self in a single spontaneous incident, prompted into action by an emergency, then we should be capable of more consistent altruistic behaviour throughout our everyday lives.

Artists of all descriptions have sought to express the anguish and beauty of life. Edvard Munch's painting

Crisis? What crisis?

The Scream dramatically captures the torment of the soul. The troubled life of Vincent van Gogh led him to vibrantly sketch and paint many masterpieces that still inspire people all over the world. Poets have struggled to clothe that "something more" in words. Music has touched us deep inside - some of the composers and singer-songwriters obviously intuitive to a higher aspect of existence. Whether it is a classical masterpiece such as Beethoven's *Ninth Symphony* with its stirring *Ode to Joy* or the more modern pop and rock 'n' roll songs, many musicians have clearly been inspired. This creativity, in turn, has undoubtedly aroused special feelings in many of those who have listened and marvelled.

The growth of science and technology has been responsible for much of the pollution that threatens to severely damage our planet. But it has also brought tremendous benefits. Advances in medical techniques have literally saved lives as well as greatly alleviating suffering. Television and other media technology has allowed millions to see images of famine and war, together with the wonders of the natural world and achievements of gold medallists in sport. It has at least brought knowledge and awareness of international affairs to the mass population - even if there is a tendency for much of the audience to still remain partly detached from the actual reality. Faster means of available transportation has greatly enhanced our capacity for global experience and a wider scope of achievement. Air travel has helped make the world a smaller place through providing greater accessibility. Automated machinery has made certain jobs safer and easier. Perhaps most importantly, recent technological developments now allow more of us greater freedom of expression in our chosen life pursuits - and this opens up huge potential for the future.....

So is life on Earth getting better or worse? We can certainly say that many of the same old problems still plague us - especially those arising from selfishness - together with a number of new complications. There is no doubt that the magnitude of the overall crisis is staggering and requires serious attention. It is also true to say that part of human nature - and the increased opportunities now available due to widespread education and technological advances - offer hope. Whether you are optimistic or pessimistic, it is what happens from now onwards that is important. What possible future scenarios are there?

ii. Is there a solution?

In the last few years, there has been a major swing towards democracy as the dominant system of politics. The situation could change again as new power struggles unfold, although overall this is less likely. Whereas a dictatorship or autocratic system can rule its country in a firm and decisive manner (for good or bad), a democratic government is obliged to consider the wishes of the people. If the representatives fail to satisfy the people in their duty of representing, they might not be re-elected. This produces a tendency to follow policies which are acceptable to the majority. Democracy therefore usually reflects rather than influences the desires of the people. In the absence of an unusually strong leader, democratic government at best realistically offers the hope of trying to contain the problems, rather than seriously expecting to solve them. There is also a greater concern to look after national interests first and foremost, considering international affairs second. It is perhaps unwise, therefore, to look for a definite solution from governments.

Technology continues to advance at a fast pace. New developments will probably bring certain benefits - but the spread of older aspects of industrialisation throughout the less wealthy countries may unfortunately add to the already alarming environmental problems. In the long-term, manufacturers will be forced by necessity to make their products more energy-efficient and less polluting. But how bad will the global situation become before any radical changes worldwide are seen as imperative at all cost? And it is unrealistic to expect that science and technology will devise anything to tackle the fundamental problem of human greed and selfishness.

A total shift in perspective is the only real solution to our apparently deepening crisis. Instead of thinking and acting in the current self-preoccupied ways, we need a broader, all-embracing attitude and approach. This will only be achieved through a significant transformation of consciousness. We need to unlock and release our full potential. Then and only then will there be an indisputable caring for the whole planet, instead of today's hypocrisy and division.

We need to rise to the challenge and re-educate ourselves. By necessity, this must be done individually. If enough people are willing to carry through the required expansion of consciousness, this alone will set up a positive example for others to quickly follow. The system will then adapt accordingly, re-adjusting in line with public expectations. It is unnecessary for individuals to achieve full consciousness in the short-term, although a major swing to this end of the scale is demanded in a significant number of people. To stimulate a fundamental worldwide movement away from the present selfish way of being will be extraordinarily difficult but not impossible. It is our best hope.

Individuals from every section of society need to initially respond. Having shaken off a significant proportion of their own mental blinkers and opened up their hearts to a large degree, these first pioneers will then have to start to speak out. If they persist, others will listen and start their own inner process of re-orientation towards a greater unity of purpose. There must be clarity and practicality. A "no-nonsense" approach will hopefully avoid the pitfalls of partition. There can be no room for any hidden agendas based on self-promotion. The goal of true renewal of mind and spirit must be paramount, with any remaining differences put aside. We need to start a peaceful and pragmatic revolution based on genuine non-selfish action. The potential benefits of such a fundamental change will have to be carefully explained to the mass population.

Good intentions or idealistic thinking alone will miserably fail. It will take much hard work to achieve any meaningful early signs of success. Anyone willing to help initiate this switch of emphasis from self to whole will first need to have started with their own inner transformation of consciousness. Once well under way, this expansion of understanding and caring must be at least maintained. This potential within us all must not be dressed up with unnecessary beliefs or terminology. What is urgently called for is a genuine meeting of minds and hearts, with no division through differences of personal or institutional ideology. And there must be practical down-to-earth action.

Collectively, we should be able to devise straightforward solutions for most of the problems in our world that urgently have to be faced. Simplicity and a direct approach should be applied whenever possible to deal with the basic issues. We need to return to fundamentals and build on these step by step, always aware that a re-adjustment from selfishness to non-selfishness is the key. If enough people recognise this way forward and are prepared to translate their insight into real action with sincere dedication, then there will be a gradual but definite awakening to our dormant capacity. We will no longer waste our time, energy, and ability. We will sensibly use our resources for the good of all. Appropriate action will replace ineffective belief as our new measuring stick of success. Petty distractions will slowly but surely lose their current importance in society, as more balanced lifestyles emerge. Creative concern will replace our present consuming wasteful- ness. As yet unrealised possibilities will unfold through unlocking and using our full potential. Development of consciousness will produce the next major step forward in human evolution.

EPILOGUE:

WHAT NEXT?

This is almost the end of the book, so what are you going to do next? If these words have made sense to you, will they prompt any significant difference in your life? Or will they merge into the many other influences that constantly compete for your attention - forgetfulness and distractions gradually dimming any spark of awareness?

What you have read contains a precise and practical blueprint for transforming consciousness. The formula must be followed exactly. You - the dreamer - have to awaken from your own dreaming.....and this is the problem. How do you turn that which is presently obscure into sharp clarity?

Remember that the time to make decisions is now. If you understand at least some of what I am saying, do not let this opportunity slip by. Act now. Begin now. Increase your awareness.

Consider using this book as a practical guide for reference. Re-read it. Examine the words carefully as all the answers are here. If you have borrowed this copy, return it and get your own. And if it has helped you, suggest it to others. Remember that full consciousness is concerned with the caring and giving of non-selfishness.

If you are a sincere and practical person, please feel free to contact me. Should there be a need, I am willing to clarify each and every sentence describing the formula. Or if you have had a oneness experience, I would be interested to hear your account. I am likewise keen to hear from anyone who wishes to help promote the idea and application of this transformation of consciousness. Write, enclosing a 22mm x 11mm stamped addressed envelope, to:

> The Human Potential Trust
> The Oasis
> Highbrook Lane
> West Hoathly
> Sussex RH19 4PL
> England

You can stand up and make a difference.....if you want to.